TORAH PORTIONS FOR CHILDREN
Vayikra
BOOK 3: LEVITICUS

NATALEE HENRY & YEVGENIYA CALENDRILLO

TORAH PORTIONS FOR CHILDREN

Vayikra

BOOK 3: LEVITICUS

Natalee Henry & Yevgeniya Calendrillo

Copyright © Natalee Henry & Yevgeniya Calendrillo, 2023.

Printed in the United States 2023.

All rights reserved. This book may not be copied or reprinted for commercial gain or profit. No portion of this book may be reproduced, stored in a retrieval system, transmitted in any form or by any means electronic, mechanical photocopy, recording, or any other except brief quotations in printed reviews, without the prior permission of the Authors and the Publisher. Rights for publishing this book in other languages are to be in written permission by Natalee Henry and Yevgeniya Calendrillo.

Unless otherwise stated, scripture References are from the New American Standard Bible (NASB), and the Tree of Life Version.

This book is a part of the Torah for Children Curriculum. www.torah4children.net

ISBN: 978-1-66640-577-4

Acknowledgments

Thanks to Ken & Lisa Albin, and our Family and Tribe at Save The Nations for your continued love, support, and encouragement throughout our writing journey.

Special thanks to Kiwi Gomes for editing and proofreading, and all the teachers at Save The Nations who have been serving in the children's ministry teaching this curriculum.

Torah Portion Titles

1. Vayikra - He Called — Page 1
2. Tzav - Command — Page 15
3. Shemini - Eighth — Page 32
4. Tazria - She Conceives* — Page 45
5. Metzora - Leper* — Page 45
6. Acharei Mot - After the Death* — Page 60
7. Kedoshim - Holy* — Page 60
8. Emor - Speak — Page 75
9. Behar - On Mount Sinai* — Page 91
10. Bechukotai - By My Regulations* — Page 91

About the Authors — Page 108

About the Book — Page 110

* indicates that these two Torah Portions are read separately during a leap year but are combined during a regular calendar year.

NOTE TO TEACHERS/PARENTS:

Dear Teachers and Parents,

Thank you for choosing to help us equip our children in the Torah Way of the Messiah. We are grateful for you and your time of service.

Each lesson is designed as a guide for teaching the Torah Portions. We encourage you to review the lesson in advance to become familiar with the material provided and allow the Holy Spirit to give you insights for teaching the lesson.

Each lesson is structured so our children will learn from the Torah Portions, and see the connection with Yeshua (Jesus), and the work of the Holy Spirit. Our aim is not just to give information but to teach Torah principles and demonstrate how to use them in their lives.

Every lesson has a general summary of the Torah Portion for the teachers and a lesson summary for the main lesson you will teach for the Torah Portion. With each lesson, there are practical applications and questions. The questions are given at the end of the lesson, however, the teacher can incorporate the questions at any time during the lesson. The practical applications are a great way for the children to make the connection between Torah and their everyday lives.

Thanks again for your time and service in helping to equip our children in the Torah Way of the Messiah.

This book is a part of the Torah for Children Curriculum. Templates for crafts are available on our website www.torah4children.net

SUGGESTED CLASS SCHEDULE

Welcome

Practical Application Follow-up From the Last Lesson in Book 1 *(See the Practical Application Page)*

Torah Portion Lesson

Bathroom Break

Crafts

Snacks

LESSON CONTENTS

Torah Portion Name and Meaning
Torah Portion Theme
Torah Portion Outline
Lesson
- Title & Meaning
- Scriptures
- Theme
- Summary
- Lesson Discussion
- Turning Point

Practical Applications
Questions and Answer Sheet
Crafts and Instructions

Vayikra

"He Called"

Torah Portion 24: Vayikra "He Called"

Scripture Readings:

Leviticus 1:1-6:7, Isaiah 43:21-44:23, Matthew 5:23-30, Psalm 50

The name of our Torah portion this week is Vayikra which means **"He Called."** It is found in the first verse of our reading.

Leviticus 1:1-2 — Now ADONAI called to Moses and spoke to him out of the Tent of Meeting, saying: **2** "Speak to *Bnei-Yisrael*, and tell them: When anyone of you brings an offering to ADONAI, you may present your offering of livestock, from the herd or from the flock.

The Theme of the Torah Portion:

Drawing Near

Scripture for Theme

Leviticus 1:1

"Speak to the sons of Israel and say to them, 'When any man of you brings an offering to the LORD, you shall bring your offering of animals from the herd or the flock.

Torah Portion Outline

- Offerings Without Defect, **Leviticus 1:1-17**
- Matzah(Grain) Offerings, **Leviticus 2:1-16**
- Shalom (Peace) Offerings, **Leviticus 3:1-17**
- Sacrifices for Unintentional Sins, **Leviticus 4:1-31**
- Sin Offerings and Other Sins, **Leviticus 4:32-35**
- If a Soul Sins (Trespass) Offering, **Leviticus 5:1-19**
- An Offering of Restitution, **Leviticus 5:20-6:7**

LESSON SUMMARY

The last Torah Portion concluded the Book of Exodus, or Shemot which means 'name' in Hebrew. All the work for the Tabernacle was completed. When Moses saw that all the work was completed, he blessed the people. The Torah Portion ended with Moses setting up the Tabernacle and it was filled with the glory of God and not even Moses could enter.

This week's Torah Portion begins a new Book which we know as Leviticus but in Hebrew is called Vayikra (Vi-he-craw). God called Moses and told him, "Speak to the sons of Israel and say to them 'when anyone of you brings an offering to the Lord,...'" Adonai gave him instructions for the different types of offerings they should bring to Him, the purpose of the offerings, and how the offerings should be prepared. These offerings were to serve as means by which the people would draw near to God and worship Him.

God brought the children of Israel out of Egypt to be His special people. He did not want them to live like other nations. As we read through the Book of Leviticus we will learn how God taught them to live for Him as His special people.

LESSON DISCUSSION

The instructions God gave Moses for the different offerings to teach the people, were to preserve His relationship with them and for restoration when they sinned.

Leviticus 1:1-3
Then the LORD called to Moses and spoke to him from the tent of meeting, saying, **2** "Speak to the sons of Israel and say to them, 'When any man of you brings an offering to the LORD, you shall bring your offering of animals from the herd or the flock. **3** If his offering is a burnt offering from the herd, he shall offer it, a male without defect; he shall offer it at the doorway of the tent of meeting, that he may be accepted before the LORD.

Moses received instructions for:
- Burnt (Elevation) Offering
- Grain Offering
- Peace Offering
- Sin Offering
- Trespass (Offense) Offering
- Restitution (Restoring) Offering

These offerings were brought to the door of the Tabernacle to be presented to God. The priest would then offer the sacrifices of the animals and the grain offering to God for the people.

We don't have a physical Tabernacle like the children of Israel had in the wilderness, or priests to offer sacrifices for us.

The offerings were for them to draw near. God wants to be near His people. He wants to draw near to you and me.

James 4:8 — Draw near to God and He will draw near to you.

Through Yeshua, God preserves His relationship with us and provides restoration to Him from sin. Yeshua is the door for us to draw near to God.

John 10:9 — I am the door, if anyone enters through Me, he will be saved.

We don't offer animal sacrifices and grain offerings, but we offer ourselves to God; through prayer, worship, serving others, giving of our tithe, and offering.

1 Corinthians 3:16 — You are the temple of God.

No matter what we have done or how badly we hurt God, He always wants us to come to him. Whenever we sin we can draw near to Him and ask for His forgiveness.

1 John 1:9 — If we confess our sins God is faith and just to forgive us.

TURNING POINT:

PASS OVER THE LEAVEN OR HONEY, MY GRAIN OFFERING!

In less than two weeks, we will be celebrating the Feast of Passover, Unleavened Bread, and Firstfruits. During this season of celebration, we are commanded to remove all the leavened products from our homes. By obeying this command we are drawing near to God.

In this week's Torah portion, we begin to learn about the offerings God commanded the children of Israel to present to Him. With these offerings, the children of Israel drew near to God. The children of Israel were commanded to bring their offerings to the door of the Tent of Meeting to be presented to God.

One of the offerings they were commanded to bring was called the 'grain offering.' The grain offering is also presented as a Firstfruits offering. This type of offering could be prepared and presented in three different ways; baked, cooked on a griddle, or cooked in a pot. One specific thing about the grain offering is that no matter how you prepared the offering it could not have any leaven or honey in it.

Leviticus 1: 4-12
He is to lay his hand upon the head of the burnt offering, and it will be accepted on his behalf to make atonement for him. **5** He is to slaughter the young bull before ADONAI; and the sons of Aharon, the *cohanim*, are to present the blood. They are to splash the blood against all sides of the altar, which is by the entrance to the tent of meeting. **6** He is to skin the burnt offering and cut it in pieces. **7** The descendants of Aharon the *cohen* are to put fire on the altar and arrange wood on the fire. **8** The sons of Aharon, the *cohanim*, are to arrange the pieces, the head and the fat on the wood which is on the fire on the altar. **9** He is to wash the entrails and lower parts of the legs with water, and the *cohen* is to cause all of it to go up in smoke on the altar as a burnt offering; it is an offering made by fire, a fragrant aroma for ADONAI. **10** "If his offering is from the flock, whether from the sheep or from the goats, for a burnt offering, he must offer a male without defect. **11** He is to slaughter it on the north side of the altar

before *ADONAI*; and the sons of Aharon, the *cohanim*, are to splash its blood against all sides of the altar. **12** He is to cut it into pieces, and the *cohen* is to arrange them with the head and fat on the wood which is on the fire on the altar.

God wants us to draw near to Him but we must know how to draw near to Him. We cannot come to Him any way we feel like it.

Leaven and honey represent the things that taste and feel good to us. We are to make a conscious choice to put away the things in our lives that make us feel good, or taste good to us, and to present ourselves to God when He wants us to draw near to Him.

James 4:8 — Draw near to God and He will draw near to you.

PRACTICAL APPLICATIONS

Drawing near to God!
Discuss with your parents what drawing near to God means to them and how they spend time drawing near to Him. What does drawing near to God mean in the following areas:
- Prayer
- Worship
- Serving Others
- Reading Torah
- Tithe and Offering

FOLLOW-UP FROM THE LAST TORAH PORTION
Ask who wants to share from last week's practical application

Honor the Shabbat

FOR CHILDREN 4-6 YEARS OLD

Help your mom prepare for Shabbat this week.

FOR CHILDREN 7-12 YEARS OLD
Help your mom prepare for Shabbat this week.

QUESTIONS - TEACHERS ANSWER KEY

1. Which Book of the Bible is called Shemot in Hebrew?
Exodus

2. What was the purpose of the offerings?
For the people to draw near to God

3. What is another name for the burnt offering?
Elevation

4. Where should the people bring the offering?
To the door of the Tent of Meeting

5. Who offered the sacrifices of the offering to God?
Aaron's sons

6. Name three of the offerings presented.
Burnt offering, Grain Offering, Peace Offering, Sin Offering, Trespass offering, Restitution Offering

7. Where does the presence of God dwell today?
In those who believe in Yeshua.

8. How can we draw near to God?
Worshiping, praying, serving others, reading Torah, giving tithe and offerings

9. **What is the name of the Book our Torah Portion begins?**
Leviticus / Vayikra

10.**How many books of the Torah have we studied so far?**
Two (2) Genesis (B'resheet) and Exodus (Shemot)

QUESTIONS - CHILDREN'S COPY

1. Which Book of the Bible is called Shemot in Hebrew?

2. What was the purpose of the offerings?

3. What is another name for the burnt offering?

4. Where should the people bring the offering?

5. Who offered the sacrifices of the offering to God?

6. Name three of the offerings presented.

7. Where does the presence of God dwell today?

8. How can we draw near to God?

9. What is the name of the Book our Torah Portion begins?

10. How many books of the Torah have we studied so far?

CRAFTS SUPPLIES FOR THE TORAH PORTION VAYIKRA

SUPPLIES:
1. 12"x12" Color Cardstock
2. Gold Cardstock
3. White Printing Paper
4. Markers/Pencils/Crayons
5. Gold Tissue Paper
6. Gold Gems
7. Red and Orange Construction Paper
8. Flame Stickers
9. Glue Sticks and Glue

CRAFTS: INTRODUCTION TO LEVITICUS!

1. Children will paste a pre-cut gold altar of sacrifice at the bottom center of 12" by 12" cardstock paper.

2. They will glue the top portion of the altar right on top as shown.

3. With glue sticks, they will glue gold strips of tissue paper around the altar, as shown.

4. They will stick a few gold gems at the top strip.

5. Children will glue orange flame on top of red flame, and then glue that on top of the altar. The altar portion is complete!

6. Now the kids will color in the word "Leviticus" title drawn by professional graffiti artist Joel Calendrillo.

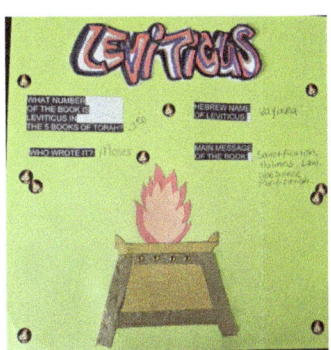

7. They will paste the title at the top center of the page.

8. Then they will glue 4 questions about the Book of Leviticus and write the answers with pencils.

9. The last step is to put flame stickers around the page.

Tzav

"Command"

Torah Portion 25: Tzav "Command"

Scripture Readings:
Leviticus 6:8-8:36, Malachi 3:4-24, Matthew 17:9-13, Psalm 107

The title of this week's Torah Portion is **"Tzav"** which means **"command"**. It is found in the second verse of our Torah reading.

Leviticus 8:2
"Command Aaron and his sons, saying, 'This is the law for the burnt offering: the burnt offering itself *shall remain* on the hearth on the altar all night until the morning, and the fire on the altar is to be kept burning on it.

The Theme of the Torah Portion:

Keep the fire Burning

Scripture for Theme

Leviticus 6:12-13 NASB

The fire on the altar shall be kept burning on it. It shall not go out, but the priest shall burn wood on it every morning; and he shall lay out the burnt offering on it, and offer up in smoke the fat portions of the peace offerings on it. **13** Fire shall be kept burning continually on the altar; it is not to go out.

Torah Portion Outline

- Law of the Burnt (Olah/Elevation) Offering, **Leviticus 6:8-13**
- Law of the Sin Offering, **Leviticus 6:24-30**
- Law of the Trespass Offering, **Leviticus 7:1-10**
- Law of the Peace Offering, **Leviticus 7:11-21**
- Fat and Blood are Forbidden to be Eaten, **Leviticus 7:22-27**
- The Portion for Aaron and His Sons, **Leviticus 7:27-38**
- Aaron and His Sons are Consecrated, **Leviticus 8:1-36**

LESSON SUMMARY

In last week's Torah Portion, Moses received instructions from God. He received instructions for different types of offerings to present to the Adonai. In this week's Torah Portion, God speaks to Moses once more. He commanded Moses to speak to Aaron and his sons about their duties as priests of Adonai. They are to minister before Him and for the people. These duties they carried out for the offerings that were presented to Adonai by Aaron or his sons. They were commanded to keep the fire on the altar burning day and night. This is where the sacrifices for burnt offerings were presented. They could not let the fire go out. The priests were also given a share of the offerings they presented. They were given the remaining portion of the grain offering and the meat from the sin and guilt offering. A special share was given to the priest who offered the peace offering. Only the family of the priest who were ritually clean could eat from the share given to them.

Aaron and his sons were to present an offering to Adonai on the day they were consecrated (anointed) to serve as priests. A command was also given that no one should eat the blood of any animal, bird, or flesh that touched an unclean thing. Adonai commanded Moses to tell the people not to eat of the fat of a bull, sheep, or goat that is offered to Him, or an animal injured by another animal.

Aaron and his sons were consecrated as priests at the door of the Tent of Meeting before all the people just as Adonai commanded Moses. They were washed before all the people, and then Moses put the priestly garments on them. Moses also anointed the Tabernacle and all the furnishings that were in it with the anointing oil. Moses sprinkled the altar, all its utensils, basin, and the base seven times with the oil to consecrate them.

Moses did all that Adonai commanded him, to consecrate Aaron and his sons, and the Tabernacle. Aaron and his sons offered their offerings to Adonai and ate the portion that belonged to them. Moses commanded them to remain at the tent door for seven days until the days of their consecration were over.

LESSON DISCUSSION

It had been two years since Adonai brought the children of Israel out of Egypt, just as He had promised Abraham. The people were gathered as a nation unto Adonai in the wilderness. We have been learning about their journey, their mistakes, and God's mercy and grace toward them. God gave Moses all the instructions and commands for building the Tabernacle, the Tabernacle furnishings, the priestly garments, and the Torah.

All the work had been completed and the priest and the tabernacle were consecrated for service. The people were about to enter a new way of life with Aaron and his sons serving as Priests to Adonai on behalf of the people.

There are two interesting commands given in this week's Torah reading:
1. The priests were to keep the fire on the altar burning for the sacrifices ~~burning~~.
2. Moses had to gather all the people together then wash Aaron and his sons with water and dress them in their priestly garments.

Keep the fire burning!
The fire on the altar was started by Adonai Himself after the sacrifice offering was put on the altar, but it was the priest's job to keep the fire burning day and night. They were to present an offering in the morning and the evening.

Leviticus 6:8-9
The LORD said to Moses: **9** "Give Aaron and his sons this command: 'These are the regulations for the burnt offering: The burnt offering is to remain on the altar hearth throughout the night, till morning, and the fire must be kept burning on the altar.

Leviticus 6:12-13

The fire on the altar must be kept burning; it must not go out. Every morning the priest is to add firewood and arrange the burnt offering on the fire and burn the fat of the fellowship offerings on it. **13** The fire must be kept burning on the altar continuously; it must not go out.

Naked and not ashamed!

Aaron and his sons were chosen by God to serve but they had to be naked before God and the people before they could wear the priestly garments.

Leviticus 8:5-13

Moses said to the congregation, "This is the thing which the LORD has commanded to do." **6** Then Moses had Aaron and his sons come near and washed them with water. **7** He put the tunic on him and girded him with the sash, and clothed him with the robe and put the ephod on him; and he girded him with the artistic band of the ephod, with which he tied *it* to him. **8** He then placed the breastpiece on him, and in the breastpiece he put the Urim and the Thummim. **9** He also placed the turban on his head, and on the turban, at its front, he placed the golden plate, the holy crown, just as the LORD had commanded Moses. **10** Moses then took the anointing oil and anointed the tabernacle and all that was in it, and consecrated them. **11** He sprinkled some of it on the altar seven times and anointed the altar and all its utensils, and the basin and its stand, to consecrate them. **12** Then he poured some of the anointing oil on Aaron's head and anointed him, to consecrate him. **13** Next Moses had Aaron's sons come near and clothed them with tunics, and girded them with sashes and bound caps on them, just as the LORD had commanded Moses.

Can you imagine how Aaron and his sons felt when they were naked before all the people? What if they had said we don't want to stand before all the people?

How would you feel if God asked you to do something that would make you feel uncomfortable?

Following God's plan for us is not about how we feel but obeying His commands.

God's commands are not always easy. Sometimes we get uncomfortable because it makes us look different from our families and friends. If we are obedient to follow God's commands we will experience His love and protection in our lives.

We have the fire (light) of God in our lives through Yeshua, our High Priest.

John 8:12
Jesus spoke to the people once more and said, "I am the light of the world. If you follow me, you won't have to walk in darkness, because you will have the light that leads to life."

Hebrews 4:14
So then, since we have a great High Priest who has entered heaven, Jesus the Son of God, let us hold firmly to what we believe.

How do we keep the light of Yeshua burning in our lives? Give kids an opportunity to share their thoughts.

Here are ways we can keep the light of Yeshua burning *(teacher can add to the list):*
1. Prayer
2. Praise and Worship
3. Honoring the Shabbat
4. Keeping the Feast Days
5. Depend on the Ruach HaKodesh (Holy Spirit) to Lead You
6. Read and Study the Torah
7. Obey God's Commands
8. Acts of Kindness

TURNING POINT:
RARE MEATS AND FATTY SHEEP!

In this week's Torah portion, Moses received instructions for priestly duties to command Aaron and his sons. God also gave Moses specific instructions for all the children of Israel.

Leviticus 7: 22-27 NASB
Then the LORD spoke to Moses, saying, **23** "Speak to the sons of Israel, saying, 'You shall not eat any fat *from* an ox, a sheep or a goat. **24** Also the fat of *an animal* which dies and the fat of an animal torn *by beasts* may be put to any other use, but you must certainly not eat it. **25** For whoever eats the fat of the animal from which an offering by fire is offered to the LORD, even the person who eats shall be cut off from his people. **26** You are not to eat any blood, either of bird or animal, in any of your dwellings. **27** Any person who eats any blood, even that person shall be cut off from his people.'"

When was the last time you wanted to go out with your friends and your parents said no? Did they give you a reason? Did the reason they gave you make any sense to you or not?

God's commands are like that sometimes. He gives us commands without explaining why. Some commands don't make any sense to us.

Does that mean we should not obey His commands? Of course not!

Even the commandments we do not understand are given to protect us and our relationship with God. It is always best to obey!

PRACTICAL APPLICATIONS
Keeping the fire (light) of Yeshua burning!

FOR CHILDREN 4-6 YEARS OLD

Ask your parent(s) to teach you how to pray.

FOR CHILDREN 7-12 YEARS OLD

Here are ways we can keep the light of Yeshua burning
1. Prayer
2. Praise & Worship
3. Honoring the Shabbat
4. Keeping the Feast Days
5. Depend on the Ruach HaKodesh (Holy Spirit) to Lead You
6. Read and Study the Torah
7. Obey God's Commands
8. Acts of Kindness

From the list above, ask yourself, which of these makes me feel uncomfortable in front of others? Write it down, then pray and ask the Ruach HaKodesh (Holy Spirit) to give you the boldness to do it and honor God.

FOLLOW-UP FROM THE LAST TORAH PORTION
Ask who wants to share from last week's practical application.

Drawing near to God!
Discuss with your parents what drawing near to God means to them and how they spend time drawing near to Him. What does drawing near to God mean in the following areas: Prayer, Worship, Serving others, Reading the Torah, Tithing, and Offerings?

QUESTIONS - TEACHERS ANSWER KEY

1. **How long were Aaron and his sons commanded to remain at the tent door to complete their consecration?**
   7 (seven) days and nights

2. **How often were the sacrifices of the burnt offering presented on the altar?**
   Evening and Morning

3. **Who was consecrated with anointing oil?**
   Aaron

4. **What was the command given to Aaron and his sons about the fire on the altar?**
   Keep it burning, don't let it go out

5. **How many times did Moses sprinkle the altar with the anointing oil?**
   7 (seven) times

6. **What were the people forbidden to eat?**
   Fat of animals, and meat with blood

7. **Why do you think it is sometimes uncomfortable for us to obey God's commandments?**
   (answer varies based on children's understanding)

8. **Who is our High Priest?**
   Yeshua

9. **How can we keep the light (fire) of Yeshua burning in our lives?** *(answer varies) (Use as reference: Praying, Praising and Worshiping, Honoring the Shabbat, Keeping the Feast Days, depending on the Ruach HaKodesh (Holy Spirit) to lead you, Reading and studying Torah, Obeying God's commands, and Acts of Kindness*

10. **How were Aaron and his sons prepared for their duties?**
    They were washed with water, then dressed in their priestly garments, and anointed with oil.

QUESTIONS - CHILDREN'S COPY

1. How long were Aaron and his sons commanded to remain at the tent door to complete their consecration?

2. How often were the sacrifices of the burnt offering presented on the altar?

3. Who was consecrated with anointing oil?

4. What was the command given to Aaron and his sons about the fire on the altar?

5. How many times did Moses sprinkle the altar with the anointing oil?

6. What were the people forbidden to eat?

7. Why do you think it is sometimes uncomfortable for us to obey God's commandments?

8. Who is our High Priest?

9. How can we keep the light (fire) of Yeshua burning in our lives?

10. How were Aaron and his sons prepared for their duties?

CRAFTS SUPPLIES FOR THE TORAH PORTION TZAV

SUPPLIES:
1. 12"x12" Colored Cardstock
2. Brown Construction Paper
3. White Cardstock
4. Blue Construction Paper
5. Gold, Purple, Red, Blue Markers or Pencils
6. Magenta/Purple and Gold Sequins
7. Colorful Gems
8. Doll Eyes
9. Glue and Glue Sticks

CRAFTS: THE PRIESTLY GARMENTS

1. Children will glue the paper doll at the center of 12" by 12" cardstock.
2. They will glue the white robe on top.

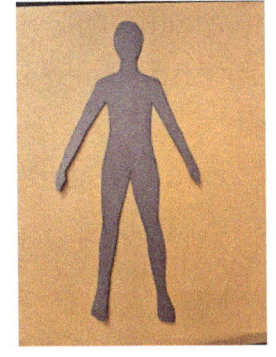 

3. Then the blue robe.
4. They will color in the ephod with gold, red, blue, and purple colors. Glue it on top.

5. Then they will glue the gold breastplate.
6. They will color the belt with gold, red, blue, and purple colors. Glue at the waist.
7. Then they will put small drops of glue at the hem of the blue robe as shown and glue magenta/purple and gold sequins there.

8. Then add 2 black gems (if they don't have black gems, they could take clear gems and color them in black) and place them at the shoulders.
9. They will take colored gems and place them at the breastpiece, as close as possible to the original example!
10. To finish it, they will put the white turban on top of his head, the beard, and 2 doll eyes.

 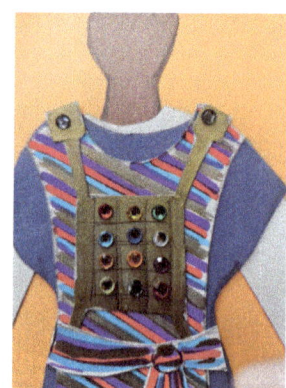

The Priest is done!!

Shemini

"Eighth"

Torah Portion 26: Shemini "Eighth"

Scripture Readings:
Leviticus 9:1-11:47, 2 Samuel 6:1-7:17, Matthew 3:11-17, Psalm 128

The title of this week's Torah Portion is **"Shemini"** which means **"eighth"**. It is found in the first verse of our Torah reading.

Leviticus 9:1 TLV
Now it happened on the eighth day that Moses called Aaron, his sons, and the elders of Israel.

The Theme of the Torah Portion:
Holy and Unholy

Scripture for Theme

Leviticus 9:8-11 TLV

Adonai spoke to Aaron saying: **9** "Do not drink wine or fermented drink, neither you nor your sons with you, when you go into the Tent of Meeting, so that you do not die. This is to be a statute forever throughout your generations. **10** You are to make a distinction between the holy and the common and between the unclean and the clean. **11** And you are to teach Bnei-Yisrael all the statutes which Adonai has spoken to them through Moses."

Torah Portion Outline

- Aron and His Sons Begin Their Priestly Duties, **Leviticus 9:1-24**
- Nadab and Abihu Offer Profane Fire, **Leviticus 10:1-7**
- Conduct for the Priest, **Leviticus 10:8-19**
- Permitted and Forbidden Foods, **Leviticus 11:1-23**
- Ritual PurityLaws, **Leviticus 11:24-47**

LESSON SUMMARY

This week's Torah portion is a continuation of the previous Torah reading, Tzav. In the last Torah portion, Tzav we learned about the consecration of the Tabernacle, Aaron, and his sons for the priesthood. The Torah reading ended with the command for Aaron and his sons to remain at the door of the Tent of Meeting for seven days to complete their consecration. This week's Torah reading begins on the eighth day, the day after their consecration was completed.

Aaron and his sons began their priestly duties on the eighth day. They were commanded to bring offerings and sacrifices to Adonai on the altar. Aaron gathered all the people and presented the offerings as Adonai commanded him. Aaron put the sacrifices on the altar then fire came down from the presence of Adonai and consumed the offerings on the altar. All the people witnessed the presence of the Lord.

Two of Aaron's sons, Nadab and Abihu brought unauthorized fire in their incense to present to Adonai on the altar. Fire came down from the presence of Adonai and consumed them, and they died in the presence of Adonai. Aaron was silent. He could not mourn for his sons. Adonai told Aaron and his other sons, Eleazar and Ithamar, not to drink any wine or strong drink before going into the Tent of Meeting.

In this Torah reading God also gave the laws concerning clean and unclean foods, animals for us to eat, and how to remain pure for Him.

LESSON DISCUSSION
Clean and Unclean

Leviticus 11:1-23 (Common English Bible)
The LORD said to Moses and Aaron: **2** Say to the Israelites: These are the creatures that you are allowed to eat from the land animals: **3** You can eat any animal that has divided hoofs, completely split, and that rechews food. **4** But of animals that rechew food and have divided hoofs you must not eat the following: the camel—though it rechews food, it does not have divided hoofs, so it is unclean for you; **5** the rock badger—though it rechews food, it does not have divided hoofs, so it is unclean for you; **6** the hare—though it rechews food, it does not have divided hoofs, so it is unclean for you; **7** the pig—though it has completely divided hoofs, it does not rechew food, so it is unclean for you. **8** You must not eat the flesh of these animals or touch their dead bodies; they are unclean for you. **9** You are allowed to eat the following from all water animals: You may eat anything in the water that has fins and scales, whether in sea or stream. **10** But anything in the seas or streams that does not have fins and scales—whether it be any of the swarming creatures in the water or any of the other living creatures in the water—is detestable to you **11** and must remain so. You must not eat their flesh, and you must detest their dead bodies. **12** Anything in the water that does not have fins or scales is detestable to you. **13** Of the birds, the following are the ones you must detest—they must not be eaten; they are detestable: the eagle, the black vulture, the bearded vulture, **14** the kite, any kind of falcon, **15** any kind of raven, **16** the eagle owl, the short-eared owl, the long-eared owl, any kind of hawk, **17** the tawny owl, the fisher owl, the screech owl, **18** the white owl, the scops owl, the osprey, **19** the stork, any kind of heron, the hoopoe, and the bat. **20** Any flying insect that walks on four feet is detestable to you, **21** but you can eat four-footed flying insects that have jointed legs above their feet with which they hop on the ground. **22** Of these you can eat the following: any kind of migrating locust, any kind of bald locust, any kind of cricket, and any

kind of grasshopper. **23** But every other flying insect that has four feet is detestable to you.

Why is it important for us to eat clean foods?

Adonai declares that we are to be holy for He is holy.

Leviticus 11:44 (CEB) — I am the Lord your God. You must keep yourselves holy and be holy, because I am holy.

He gives us specific instructions on how to live a holy life. Eating foods that He tells us to eat is one way we can live holy and be holy like Him.

God wants us to draw near to Him not just with our offerings but in our daily routine. Eating foods permitted by Him and avoiding unclean foods allows us to draw near to Him.

TURNING POINT:

Fire You Desire!

Leviticus 10:1-3

Now Nadab and Abihu, two of Aaron's sons, each took an incense pan. They put fire and incense on them and offered unauthorized fire before the LORD, which he had not commanded them. **2** Then fire flew out from before the LORD and devoured them, and they died before the LORD. **3** Moses said to Aaron, "When the LORD said, 'I will show that I am holy among those near me, and before all the people I will manifest my glorious presence,' this is what he meant!" But Aaron was silent. Can you imagine seeing your brother or sister die while doing their job, then you have to take their place? Wow! What a hard and painful task. This is what happened to Eleazar and Ithamar. After the death of Nadab and Abihu, their brothers, they were now responsible to serve alongside their father Aaron as priests.

No doubt the deaths of their brothers served as a constant reminder to them to always do the right thing. It also had to be emotionally painful for them. What if they were afraid and didn't want to do their job? Does this mean they too were at risk of dying? This is not the character of Adonai. He does not take pleasure in killing His people. Nadab and Abihu did something that Adonai, God did not require. They did not honor God in their actions.

Learning from the mistakes of others can spare us from experiencing pain. As you grow older, you will be tempted to live life "on your own terms." May the experiences of your parents, your friends, and your siblings be a reminder to you to always choose to do what pleases Adonai.

PRACTICAL APPLICATIONS

Make a decision today that you will eat only clean foods.

FOLLOW-UP FROM THE LAST TORAH PORTION
Ask who wants to share from last week's practical application

Keeping the fire (light) of Yeshua burning!

FOR CHILDREN 4-6 YEARS OLD

Ask your parent(s) to teach you how to pray.

FOR CHILDREN 7-12 YEARS OLD

Here are ways we can keep the light of Yeshua burning
1. Prayer
2. Praise and Worship
3. Honoring the Shabbat
4. Keeping the Feast Days
5. Depending on the Ruach HaKodesh (Holy Spirit) to Lead You
6. Reading and Studying Torah
7. Obeying God's Commands
8. Acts of Kindness

From the list above, ask yourself, which of these makes me feel uncomfortable in front of others? Write it down, then pray and ask the Ruach HaKodesh (Holy Spirit) to give you the boldness to do it and honor God.

QUESTIONS - TEACHERS ANSWER KEY

1. How many days did it take for Aaron and his son's consecration?

seven

2. Where did the fire come from to devour the offering on the altar?

The presence of Adonai

3. On which day did Aaron and his sons begin their duties as priests?

Eighth day

4. What were the priests not allowed to drink before they ministered in the Tent of Meeting?

Wine or strong drink

5. Name Aaron's sons who died.

Nadab and Abihu

6. Why did Aaron's sons die?

They offered unauthorized fire in the presence of Adonai

7. According to Leviticus 11:44 why did God say we should be holy?

He is our God and He is holy

8. What kind of land animals are considered clean to eat?

Those with split hooves and rechews their food

9. What kind of sea creatures are considered unclean?

Those without fins and scales

10. Why do we eat only clean foods?

To be holy like Adonai

QUESTIONS - CHILDREN'S COPY

1. How many days did it take for Aaron and his son's consecration?

2. Where did the fire come from to devour the offering on the altar?

3. On which day did Aaron and his sons begin their duties as priests?

4. What were the priests not allowed to drink before they ministered in the Tent of Meeting?

5. Name Aaron's sons who died.

6. Why did Aaron's sons die?

7. According to Leviticus 11:44 why did God say we should be holy?

8. What kind of land animals are considered clean to eat?

9. What kind of sea creatures are considered unclean?

10. Why do we eat only clean foods?

CRAFTS SUPPLIES FOR THE TORAH PORTION SHEMINI

SUPPLIES:
1. 12x12" Cardstock of Various Colors
2. Print out paper
3. Glue Sticks
4. Markers/Pencils/Crayons
5. Stapler

CRAFTS: CLEAN AND UNCLEAN ANIMALS!

1. Children will get 2 12x12" cardstock papers and cutouts of clean and unclean animals in each category (animals, fish, birds, insects, crawling things) as well as Scripture verses.

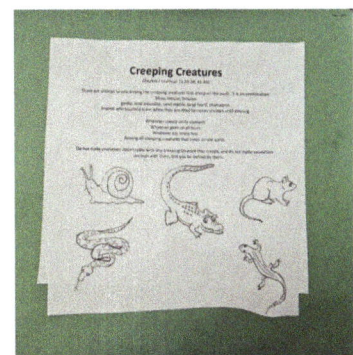

2. They will glue the cutouts as the original.
3. Mark the categories as clean or unclean.
4. Then they will color <u>at the end</u>.
5. Staple two cardstock pages together.

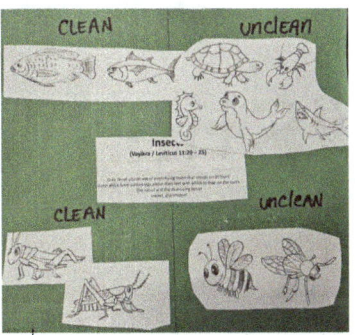

This will serve as a guide for the future!

Tazria-Metzora

"She Conceives & Leper"

Torah Portion 27 & 28:
Tazria-Metzora "She Conceives & Leper"

Scripture Readings:
Tazria: Leviticus 12:1-13:59, Isaiah 66:1-24, Mark 9:40-50, Psalms 106

Metzora: Leviticus 24:1-15:33, 2 Kings 4:42-5:19, Matthew 8:1-4, Psalms 120

The title of this week's Torah portion is a double portion, Tazria - Metzora. The Hebrew word **"Tazria"** means **"conceives",** and it is found in Leviticus 12:2. **"Metzora"** is the Hebrew word translated as **"leper."** and it is found in Leviticus 14:2.

Leviticus 12:2 — "Speak to Bnei-Yisrael, instructing: If a woman **conceives** and bears a male child, then she will be unclean for seven days, as in the days of her niddah she will be unclean.

Leviticus 14:2 — "This shall be the law of the **leper** in the day of his cleansing. Now he shall be brought to the priest.

The Theme of the Torah Portion:
Examine Me!

Scripture for Theme

Leviticus 13:3
The priest will examine the infection on the skin.

Torah Portion Outline

- Childbirth and Purification Laws, **Leviticus 12:1-12**
- Tzarat of the Skin, **Leviticus 13:1-28**
- Tzarat of the Head and Face, **Leviticus 13:29-46**
- Tzarat on Garments, **Leviticus 13:47-59**
- Purification and Offerings for Metzora, **Leviticus 14:1-32**
- Tzarat in Your Houses and the Purification Law, **Leviticus 14:33-57**
- Purification From Body Discharges for Males, **Leviticus 15:1-18**
- Purification From Body Discharges for Females, **Leviticus 15:19-30**
- Separation From Contamination, **Leviticus 15:31-33**

LESSON SUMMARY

The name of this Torah portion is Tazria-Metzora because it consists of two Torah portions; Tazria and Metzora. Tazria which means 'she conceives' is found in Leviticus 12:2. Metzora is translated as 'leper', and is found in Leviticus 14:2. In Tazria-Metzora we learn about the laws for clean and unclean people, garments, houses, and utensils. It is a continuation of last week's Torah portion, Shemini, in which we learned about clean and unclean foods.

We are told that after giving birth a woman has a time of impurity or uncleanness. Her time of impurity after giving birth to a boy was seven days and her purification process lasted for thirty-three days. When she gave birth to a girl, she was impure for fourteen days and her purification process lasted sixty-six days. When her time of purification was complete, she was to bring an offering to the priest to present before Adonai.

Our readings also discuss the laws concerning Tzara'at, which is a supernatural plague caused by Adonai, it is known as leprosy. It can affect a person's skin, clothing, or house. If a person has a swelling, a scab, a bright spot, a boil, a burning rash that becomes a bright spot, reddish-white or white in the skin, or unusual baldness; he or she was to go to the priest to be examined. The priest declared the person unclean for seven days, then on the eighth day examined the person again. If the infected area got better then he was declared clean by the priest, but if the infection spread he was declared unclean, he or she had (leprosy) Tzara'at. The person who has Tzara'at (leprosy) plague (not a plague) had to tear his or her clothes, let loose their hair, cover their upper lip, and cry "Unclean! Unclean!!" The person also had to dwell outside the camp until the plague was healed and the priest declared him or her clean. Anyone affected with Tzara'at (leprosy) had to present an offering to Adonai and be cleansed by the priest for purification, wash themselves and their clothes before they were declared clean and could enter the camp.

The priests were also given instructions for clothes, utensils, and houses that were infected. No one with (leprosy) Tzara'at or who were impure from a bodily discharge could enter the camp. Clothes that were infected had to be burned if they still had a mark of the plague Tzara'at after washing them. If a house had a mark, everything had to be taken out before the priest could enter to examine it. A house that was contaminated with Tzara'at (leprosy) was broken down, its stones, its timber, along with all the house's mortar, and were carried out of the city into an unclean place.

LESSON DISCUSSION

The Plague of Leprosy (Tzara'at)
Leviticus 14:1-3 NASB

Then the LORD spoke to Moses and to Aaron, saying, 2 "When a man has on the skin of his body a swelling or a scab or a bright spot, and it becomes an infection of leprosy on the skin of his body, then he shall be brought to Aaron the priest or to one of his sons the priests. 3 The priest shall look at the mark on the skin of the body, and if the hair in the infection has turned white and the infection appears to be deeper than the skin of his body, it is an infection of leprosy; when the priest has looked at him, he shall pronounce him unclean.

Manifestations of Tzara'at (Leprosy)
- Swelling
- Scab
- Bright spot
- Boils
- Rash

What Makes a person unclean with the plague of Tzara'at (leprosy)?

As we read through this Torah portion we learn of the different ways that the plague of Tzara'at or leprosy could infect a person, clothes, or a house. There is no explanation for how someone would get Tzara'at or leprosy. The only time we are given a reason for the plague is when it is found in a house.

Leviticus 14:33-34 NASB

The LORD further spoke to Moses and to Aaron, saying: **34** "When you enter the land of Canaan, which I give you for a possession, and I put a mark of leprosy on a house in the land of your possession, **35** then the one who owns the house shall come and tell the priest, saying,

'*Something* like a mark *of leprosy* has become visible to me in the house.'

Why a house in Canaan?
The word Canaan in Hebrew means humiliated or humiliate, or to humble oneself.

A marked house in Canaan means that God requires humility from the owner of the house.

Can you think of a story in the Torah that God caused plagues because the people would not humble themselves? (hint Passover play)

Pharaoh would not let the children of Israel go from Egypt to serve Adonai.

What was one of the plagues that God caused to infect the people of Egypt that we see in this week's Torah portion?

God wanted Pharaoh to humble himself but he would not. He hardened his heart against God and the children of Israel.

If Pharaoh was plagued with boils, which is a form of leprosy because he refused to humble himself before God, could it be possible that a person who is infected with leprosy (Tzara'at) does not show humility before Adonai?

TURNING POINT:
Make Me Clean!

Matthew 8:1-4
When Jesus came down from the mountain, large crowds followed Him. **2** And a leper came to Him and bowed down before Him, and said, "Lord, if You are willing, You can make me clean." **3** Jesus stretched out His hand and touched him, saying, "I am willing; be cleansed." And immediately his leprosy was cleansed. **4** And Jesus said to him, "See that you tell no one; but go, show yourself to the priest and present the offering that Moses commanded, as a testimony to them."

Unclean! Unclean!, cries the leper as he makes his way toward the crowd to see Yeshua (Jesus). Did he really? Our Torah portion tells us that anyone who has leprosy (Tzara'at) should wear torn clothes, wear his hair loose and uncombed, cover his upper lip, and cry, unclean, unclean.

Can you imagine how people looked at him as he passed through the crowd? Or even the shame he felt? That did not stop him from going to Yeshua. Yeshua knew the man wanted to be healed. He also knew that according to the Torah, only the priest can declare a person clean or unclean from Tzara'at (leprosy). Yeshua honored Torah even though He was the Son of God, and He was willing to heal the leper. After healing the leper, He said to him, "Go show yourself to the priest." Only the priest could declare him clean.

Yeshua is waiting for you to come to Him! You may feel guilty and ashamed when you do something wrong, or if talk bad about a person, or if you were disciplined by your parents, or by a teacher at school. Others may say bad things about you, but just as the leper went to Yeshua to be healed, you too can go to Him for healing and forgiveness.

Are you willing to let the light of the Holy Spirit examine your heart?

Romans 8:27 The Passion Translation

"God, the searcher of the heart, knows fully our longings, yet he also understands the desires of the Spirit, because the Holy Spirit passionately pleads before God for us, his holy ones, in perfect harmony with God's plan and our destiny."

PRACTICAL APPLICATIONS

FOR CHILDREN 4-6 YEARS OLD

Pray with your parents and ask God to give you wisdom to always speak the right words.

FOR CHILDREN 7-12 YEARS OLD

Pray and ask the Holy Spirit to examine your heart and show you if there is unforgiveness towards someone. When He shows you, ask your Heavenly Father to forgive you and help you to forgive the person.

FOLLOW-UP FROM THE LAST TORAH PORTION

Ask who wants to share from last week's practical application

EATING CLEAN!

Make a decision today that you will eat only clean foods.

QUESTIONS - TEACHERS ANSWER KEY

1. **Name two ways leprosy (Tzara'at) manifests in a person's skin.**
   Swelling, Scab, Bright Spot, Boils, Rash

2. **How many days was a woman considered unclean after having a son?**
   7 days

3. **How many days are requested for a woman's purification after having a daughter?**
   66 days

4. **Who can declare a person clean or unclean?**
   The priest

5. **How many days was a woman considered unclean after having a daughter?**
   14 days

6. **Which three places can the plague of Tzara'at (leprosy) appear?**
   A person's skin, clothes, house

7. **How many days are requested for a woman's purification after having a son?**
   33 days

8. **How many days does a person remain unclean when he is first examined by the priest?**
   7 days

9. **What does a person with Tzara'at cry out?**
   Unclean, unclean!

10. **What does Canaan mean in Hebrew?**
    Humiliated, to humiliate, or to humble oneself

QUESTIONS - CHILDREN'S COPY

1. Name two ways leprosy (Tzara'at) manifests in a person's skin.

2. How many days was a woman considered unclean after having a son?

3. How many days are requested for a woman's purification after having a daughter?

4. Who can declare a person clean or unclean?

5. How many days was a woman considered unclean after having a daughter?

6. Which three places can the plague of Tzara'at (leprosy) appear?

7. How many days are requested for a woman's purification after having a son?

8. How many days does a person remain unclean when he is first examined by the priest?

9. What does a person with Tzara'at cry out?

10. What does Canaan mean in Hebrew?

CRAFTS SUPPLIES FOR TORAH PORTION TAZRIA-METZORA

1. 12x12" Cardstock
2. White Cardstock
3. Red and Orange Construction Paper
4. Orange Felt
5. Pink Felt
6. Cotton Balls
7. Paper Towels
8. Fabric Swatches
9. Pink and Yellow Paint
10. Doll Eyes
11. Glue and Glue sticks
12. Markers, Pencils

CRAFTS:

1. Children will Outline their own hands on the cardstock.
2. Glue orange and pink felt on the hand. Put a large dot with marker on top of pink felt.
3. Glue a piece of paper towel on the hand.
4. Glue cotton balls on the hand. Small piece.

5. Glue a shirt cut out on the cardstock.
6. Drop SMALL drops of pink and yellow paint on the shirt and smudge it with a cotton ball as shown. Allow it to dry.
7. Glue pre-cut flames under the shirt.

8. Glue pre-cut bald head.
9. Draw a scab on top of the head as shown.
10. Glue doll eyes.
11. Draw a sad face.

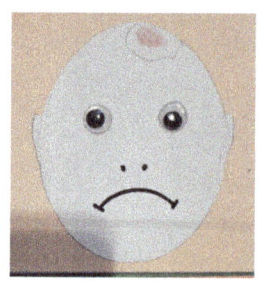

12. Color Leviticus 13 letters and glue them on the right-hand side.

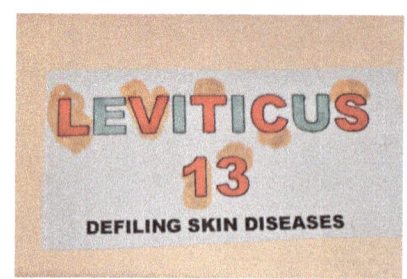

THE COMPLETE WORK

Acharei Mot-Kedoshim

"After the Death & Holy"

Torah Portion 29-30:
Acharei Mot - Kedoshim "After the Death & Holy"

Scripture Readings:
Acharei Mot: Leviticus 16:1-18:37, Ezekiel 22:1-19, Matthew 15:10-20, Psalms 26

Kedoshim: Leviticus 19:1-20:27, Amos 9:7-15, Galatians 5:13-26, Psalms 15

The title of this week's Torah portion is a double portion, Acharei Mot-Kedoshim. The Hebrew phrase **Acharei Mot** means *"After the death"* and it is found in Leviticus 16:1. **Kedoshim** is the Hebrew word translated as *"Holy"*, and it is found in Leviticus 19:2.

Leviticus 16:1 — Now the Lord spoke to Moses **after the death** of the two sons of Aaron, when they had approached the presence of the Lord and died.

Leviticus 19:2 — "Speak to all the congregation of the sons of Israel and say to them, 'You shall be holy, for I the Lord your God am holy.

The Theme of the Torah Portion:
Be Holy

Scripture for Theme

Leviticus 19:1-2 Common English Bible

The LORD said to Moses, **2** Say to the whole community of the Israelites: You must be holy, because I, the LORD your God, Am holy.

Torah Portion Outline

- After the Death of Aaron's Sons, **Leviticus 16:1-2**
- Yom Kippur Service, **Leviticus 16:3-34**
- Sacrifices Outside the Camp, **Leviticus 17:1-9**
- Do Not Eat Blood, **Leviticus 17:10-15**
- Forbidden Practices and Traditions, **Leviticus 18:1-5**
- Forbidden Relationships and Other Practices, **Leviticus 18:6-23**
- The Holiness of the Land, **Leviticus 18:24-30**
- Holiness, **Leviticus 19:1-2**
- Rejected Offerings, **Leviticus 19:3-8**
- Gifts to the Poor, **Leviticus 19:11-18**
- No Mixture, **Leviticus 19:19**
- How to Treat a Maidservant, **Leviticus 19:20-22**
- Trees, Weights, and Measures, **Leviticus 19:23-37**
- No Idol Worship, Leviticus 20:1-9
- Penalties for Forbidden Relationships, **Leviticus 20:10-22**
- Immoral Practices and Holiness, **Leviticus 20:23-27**

LESSON SUMMARY

The name of this Torah portion is Acharei Mot-Kedoshim because it consists of two Torah portions; Acharei Mot and Kedoshim. The Hebrew phrase Acharei Mot means "After the death" and it is found in Leviticus 16:1. Kedoshim is the Hebrew word translated as "Holy", and it is found in Leviticus 19:2. In Acharei Mot-Kedoshim we learn about the "holiness codes" God gave to Moses to instruct the priest and the children of Israel after the death of Aaron's sons.

After the death of Aaron's sons, God gave Moses instructions for Aaron to let him know how he should enter the Most Place. He could not enter any way he pleased. He had to follow God's instructions to enter His presence. He had to offer a sacrifice which is known as the atonement sacrifice. He also had to bathe and dress in his priestly garments; the holy tunic, the undergarment, the sash, and the turban which were all made from linen. He also offered this sacrifice on behalf of the priest and all people. Aaron was told to make an atonement sacrifice every year for himself and the children of Israel. This atonement sacrifice is the sixth feast day we honor every year on the Day of Atonement.

This week's Torah portion also covers a variety of laws regarding relationships, how to treat each other, birds, trees, the land, and giving gifts to the poor. Also, it covers Adonai's disapproval of idol worship, unholy blood sacrifices, eating meats with blood, unacceptable offerings, and a forbidden mixture of garments, seeds sown together in the field, and animals. These laws Adonai gave the children of Israel to teach them how to be holy as He is Holy.

LESSON DISCUSSION

"You shall be holy, for I the LORD your God am holy."

Leviticus 19:1-8 NASB

Then the LORD spoke to Moses, saying: **2** "Speak to all the congregation of the sons of Israel and say to them, 'You shall be holy, for I the LORD your God am holy. **3** Every one of you shall reverence his mother and his father, and you shall keep My sabbaths; I am the LORD your God. **4** Do not turn to idols or make for yourselves molten gods; I am the LORD your God. **5** 'Now when you offer a sacrifice of peace offerings to the LORD, you shall offer it so that you may be accepted. **6** It shall be eaten the same day you offer *it*, and the next day; but what remains until the third day shall be burned with fire. **7** So if it is eaten at all on the third day, it is an offense; it will not be accepted. **8** Everyone who eats it will bear his iniquity, for he has profaned the holy thing of the LORD; and that person shall be cut off from his people.

THE BIG FIVE
1. **Reverence your mother and father**
2. **Keep My Sabbaths**
3. **Do not turn to idols or make molten gods**
4. **Offer your offerings in an acceptable manner**
5. **Eat your portion of the offering at the acceptable time**

It seems strange that God would give the children of Israel a list of do's and don'ts to teach them how to be holy. Why?

Our actions are a reflection of the God we serve. God gave instructions on how to live because these will be a sign to the other nations that Israel serves the Creator God. These instructions represented the quality of God's relationship with those who choose to serve and obey Him.

SEPARATED UNTO ADONAI

Adonai was preparing the people to bring them into the land He promised to Abraham, Isaac, and Jacob. He did not want them to follow the customs, traditions, or practices of the nations He would drive out from the land for them to possess.

Leviticus 20:22-24 NASB
'You are therefore to keep all My statutes and all My ordinances and do them, so that the land to which I am bringing you to live will not spew you out. **23** Moreover, you shall not follow the customs of the nation which I will drive out before you, for they did all these things, and therefore I have abhorred them. **24** Hence I have said to you, "You are to possess their land, and I Myself will give it to you to possess it, a land flowing with milk and honey." I am the LORD your God, who has separated you from the peoples.'

Through Yeshua, we are separated unto Adonai.

2 Corinthians 6:16-18 The Message
Don't become partners with those who reject God. How can you make a partnership out of right and wrong? That's not partnership; that's war. Is light best friends with dark? Does Christ go strolling with the Devil? Do trust and mistrust hold hands? Who would think of setting up pagan idols in God's holy Temple? But that is exactly what we are, each of us a temple in whom God lives. God himself put it this way: "I'll live in them, move into them; I'll be their God and they'll be my people.
So leave the corruption and compromise; leave it for good," says God. "Don't link up with those who will pollute you. I want you all for myself. I'll be a Father to you; you'll be sons and daughters to me." The Word of the Master, God.

God wants you for Himself. Are you willing to give yourself to Him?

TURNING POINT:

"BECAUSE I SAID SO!'

Leviticus 20:22 -24 TLV (Tree of Life Version)

"Now you are to keep all My statutes and all My ordinances and do them, so that the land where I am bringing you to dwell will not vomit you out. **23** You are not to walk in the ways of the nation which I am casting out before you, for they did all these things and therefore I abhorred them. **24** But I have said to you, 'You will inherit their land and I will give it to you to possess it, a land flowing with milk and honey.' I am Adonai your God, who has set you apart from the peoples.

As we read through this week's Torah portion we see God constantly telling the people, "I Am Adonai" and "I Am Adonai Your God" as He gives them instructions for living a holy lifestyle. He makes this declaration twenty-five times (25). Yep, that's right God reminded the people twenty-five times that He is Adonai their God in this one Torah portion. Can you imagine your mom or dad saying "I am your parent" twenty-five times in one day?

Why do you think God had to remind the people who He is and His role in their lives? I believe God wanted the people to realize that these instructions should be obeyed because they are His words and not just words coming from Moses, Aaron, or the other Priests.

Have your parents ever told you, "Because I said so"? This response seems unkind and unfair when you want something and that is all you get. Do you think your parents are just mean and don't want you to have fun? It is their way of saying we are your parents and we know what is best for you. Your response is to obey and honor them even if you feel hurt.

God telling the children of Israel "I Am Adonai" and "I Am Adonai Your God" is similar to when your parents say "Because I said so." God wanted the people to know that He desired them to obey what He said, simply because He is their God. He is the one who delivered them, watched over, protected, provided for, and sheltered them.

Next time your parents say to you "Because I said so" remember God has entrusted you to their care. They are responsible for watching over, protecting, providing for, shelter, and keeping you from danger.

Leviticus 19: 3 TLV
"Each one of you is to respect his mother and his father and keep My Shabbatot (Sabbaths). I am Adonai your God.

PRACTICAL APPLICATIONS

Responding in Obedience.
Purpose in your heart to respond in obedience to your parents, and or, teachers immediately, so they do not have to tell you a second time what to do.

FOLLOW-UP FROM LAST TORAH PORTION
Ask who wants to share from last week's practical application

FOR CHILDREN 4-6 YEARS OLD

Pray with your parents and ask God to give you wisdom to always speak the right words.

FOR CHILDREN 7-12 YEARS OLD

Pray and ask the Holy Spirit to examine your heart and show you if there is unforgiveness towards someone. When He shows you, ask your Heavenly Father to forgive you and help you to forgive the person.

QUESTIONS - TEACHERS ANSWER KEY

1. **What kind of sacrifice was Aaron commanded to offer before entering the Most Holy Place?**
   Atonement

2. **For whom did Aaron make atonement?**
   Himself, his sons, and all of Israel

3. **How often was the sacrifice of atonement made to Adonai?**
   Once every year

4. **Who was the first person God promised to give land as possession?**
   Abraham

5. **What kind of material were Aaron's garments made from?**
   Linen

6. **What three things does God forbid to be mixed with different kinds?**
   Garments, animals, seeds

7. **Where did the presence of God dwell in the Tabernacle?**
   In the Most Holy Place

8. **The people were commanded not to eat meat with this?**
   Blood

9. **According to Leviticus 20:23, what did God tell Israel not to follow?**
   Customs, practices, and traditions of the nations He will drive out from the land He is giving them.

10. **As Torah-observant believers in Yeshua, what are some of the customs, practices, and traditions we do not follow?**
    Allow the kids to give their answers then share as necessary

QUESTIONS - CHILDREN'S COPY

1. What kind of sacrifice was Aaron commanded to offer before entering the Most Holy Place?

2. For whom did Aaron make atonement?

3. How often was the sacrifice of atonement made to Adonai?

4. Who was the first person God promised to give land as possession?

5. What kind of material were Aaron's garments made from?

6. What three things do God forbid to be mixed with different kinds?

7. Where does the presence of God dwell in the Tabernacle?

8. The people were commanded not to eat meat with this?

9. According to Leviticus 20:23, what did God tell Israel not to follow?

10. As Torah-observant believers in Yeshua, what are some of the customs, practices, and traditions we do not follow?

CRAFTS SUPPLIES FOR THE TORAH PORTION ACHAREI MOT-KEDOSHIM

SUPPLIES:
1. 12x12" 2 Pieces of Cardstock Attached
2. *Print color sheet templates
3. Markers/Pencils
4. Popsicle Sticks
5. Glue Sticks
6. Glue
7. Matzah Pieces
8. Fake Leaves
9. Leaves Stickers
10. Gems

*Color sheet templates are found on our website www.torah4children.net

CRAFTS: APPOINTED FEASTS OF ADONAI

Please note that this is a 2-WEEK PROJECT. Teachers in the first week, do not rush to finish it. You can focus on steps 1 through 5. If you have extra time, you can keep going to step 6.

Please collect their artwork at the end of the class. Don't allow them to take it home. will receive a 2-page cardstock booklet.

1. Glue the Appointed feasts of Adonai and 7 branch menorah in the front of the craft booklet.

2. On the inside (left-hand side), create a door out of popsicle sticks, glue a drawing of lamb, and color it. Glue and color the Passover header.
3. Mark it on top and sides with a red marker to represent blood.
4. Next to it, glue the header Feast of Unleavened Bread and glue matzah under it.

5. Under Passover, glue header First Fruits and barley Under it.
6. Next to it, glue header Shavuot, and Torah drawing.

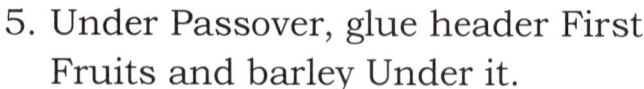

7. On the right side of the booklet, left corner, glue the header Yom Teruah and a man with a shofar drawing.
8. Next to it, glue the header Yom Kippur and Forbidden things under it.

9. On the bottom, glue the Sukkot header, and Sukkah drawing and color it. Put popsicle sticks around to represent Sukkah. Then fake leaves around it.

The Final Artwork

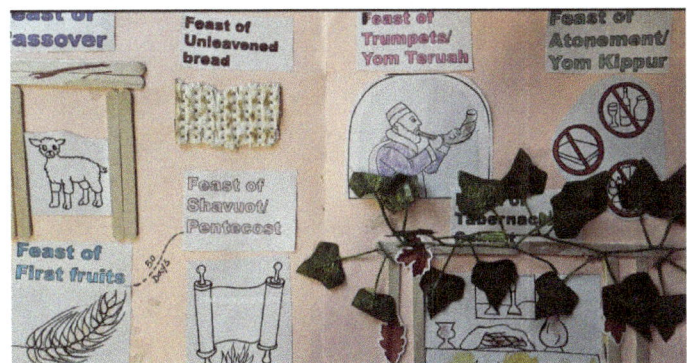

Emor

"Speak"

Torah Portion 31: Emor "Speak"

Scripture Readings:

Leviticus 21:1-24:23, Ezekiel 44:15-31, Matthew 26:59-66, Psalm 42

The title of this week's Torah Portion is **"Emor"** which means "**speak**". It is found in the first verse of our Torah reading.

Leviticus 21:1 TLV

Then Adonai said to Moses, "Speak to the kohanim, the sons of Aaron, and say to them: A kohen is not to allow himself to become unclean for the dead among his people.

The Theme of the Torah Portion:

Adonai's Appointed Times

Leviticus 23:4 NASB

'These are the appointed times of the Lord, holy convocations which you shall proclaim at the times appointed for them.

Torah Portion Outline

- Rules are Given for the Priest, **Leviticus 21:1-9**
- Rules are Given for the High Priest, **Leviticus 21:10-16**
- Birth Defects and Blemishes, **Leviticus 21:1-24**
- Protecting the Holiness of the Offerings, **Leviticus 22:1-17**
- No Blemished Animals for Offerings, **Leviticus 22:18-25**
- Do Not Profane the Name of Adonai, **Leviticus 22:26-32**
- The Feast Days of Adonai- the Sabbath, **Leviticus 23:1-3**
- Passover (Pesach), **Leviticus 23:4-8**
- Counting the Omer, **Leviticus 23:9-14**
- Shavuot (Pentecost), **Leviticus 23:15-22**
- Rosh Hashanah (Yom Terumah), **Leviticus 23:23-25**
- Yom Kippur (Day of Atonement), **Leviticus 23:26-32**
- Sukkot (Feast of Tabernacles) and Shemini Atzeres, **Leviticus 23:33-44**
- Lighting the Menorah, **Leviticus 24:1-4**
- Preparing the Table of Showbread, **Leviticus 24:5-9**
- The One Who Blasphemes the Name of Adonai, **Leviticus 24:10-23**

LESSON SUMMARY

This week's Torah Portion begins with the commands for the priests. They were; not to defile themselves except for a close relative. They could only marry women who have never been married. The High Priest, who is anointed with the holy oil to wear the holy garments (ephod, the linen turban, the belt, and the robe) should not defile himself, not even for a close relative. No priest who was born with defects or had any blemishes could serve in the Tabernacle as a priest to Adonai, but he could eat from the priests' portion. Animals chosen for offerings and sacrifices also could not have any blemishes or defects. A young animal must remain with its mother for seven days before it can be taken as an offering to Adonai. A young animal and its mother should not be offered as a sacrifice on the same day.

This Torah portion also teaches us about the feast days of Adonai which He said we are to proclaim in their season. It begins with the Sabbath day, a weekly feast. The Yearly feasts are Passover, and Unleavened Bread with the command not to have leaven (yeast) in our homes or eat any leaven for seven days. The feast of First Fruits begins the counting of the Omer; when it is commanded to bring an Omer measure of barley to the Priest. The Omer is counted for seven weeks (49 days). Shavuot is the fourth feast remembering the day Adonai gave the Torah on Mount Sinai. It is observed on the fiftieth (50th) day after counting the Omer. The Feast of Trumpets (Rosh Hashanah), also known as The Day of Atonement (Yom Kippur), is a day of repentance when we ask Adonai's forgiveness of our sins. The Feast of Sukkot (Feast of Tabernacles/Booths) is also a seven-day feast with an extra day. The first day and the eighth day are Sabbath days of rest. The children of Israel were to live in booths for seven days as a reminder that Adonai, their God, brought them out of the land of Egypt. The eighth day after Sukkot is also a special day. It is known as Shemini Atzeret.

Instructions were also given for the Menorah and Table of Showbread (Bread of the Presence). The Priest was commanded to keep the light burning so it would not go out. Twelve loaves of bread were to be set on the Table of Showbread. The Twelve Loaves represented the twelve tribes of Israel. They were set in two rows, six loaves of bread in each row, with frankincense spice as a memorial to Adonai. Every Sabbath day the priest would place fresh bread on the table. The Torah reading ends with instructions for anyone who blasphemes the name of Adonai.

LESSON DISCUSSION

Adonai's Appointed Times

Leviticus 23:1-4 NASB

he Lord spoke again to Moses, saying, **2** "Speak to the sons of Israel and say to them, 'The Lord's appointed times which you shall proclaim as holy convocations—My appointed times are these: **3** 'For six days work may be done, but on the seventh day there is a sabbath of complete rest, a holy convocation. You shall not do any work; it is a sabbath to the Lord in all your dwellings. **4** 'These are the appointed times of the Lord, holy convocations which you shall proclaim at the times appointed for them.

All the feast days are holy unto Adonai. They are Adonai's appointed times. The feast days of Adonai are celebrated during two seasons of the year, Spring and Fall. During the spring feasts, we celebrate Passover, Unleavened Bread, FirstFruits, and ends with Shavuot. The fall feast begins with; the Feast of Trumpets, also known as Rosh Hashanah. We also celebrate the Day of Atonement (Yom Kippur), Sukkot, and the Eighth day (Shemini Atzeret).

A New Beginning
Exodus 12:1-2

Now the Lord said to Moses and Aaron in the land of Egypt, 2 "This month shall be the beginning of months for you; it is to be the first month of the year to you.

Leviticus 23:5, 23-25

In the first month, on the fourteenth day of the month at twilight is the Lord's Passover. 23 Again the Lord spoke to Moses, saying, 24 "Speak to the sons of Israel, saying, 'In the seventh month on the first of the month you shall have a rest, a reminder by blowing of trumpets, a holy convocation.

Both seasons marked a new beginning for the children of Israel. While living in Egypt they had to follow the Egyptian calendar and observe their feast days. God gave them a new calendar with festivals they should celebrate to honor Him and not the gods of Egypt. Passover marks the season of redemption, a time when Adonai brought them out of Egypt and separated them for Himself. The Feast of Trumpets marks a time when they were to listen for the voice of Adonai and to draw near to Him. The Day of Atonement was to prepare their hearts for time spent in booths during Sukkot and the Eight Day.

A New Beginning With Yeshua
Galatians 3:26-29
26 For in union with the Messiah, you are all children of God through this trusting faithfulness; **27** because as many of you as were immersed into the Messiah have clothed yourselves with the Messiah, in whom **28** there is neither Jew nor Gentile, neither slave nor freeman, neither male nor female; for in union with the Messiah Yeshua, you are all one. **29** Also, if you belong to the Messiah, you are seed of Avraham and heirs according to the promise.

Through Yeshua, we inherit the promises of God as children of Abraham through faith. Like the children of Israel, we are taken from spiritual Egypt, a state of hopelessness, loneliness, fear, doubt, and death. We get to enjoy the presence of Adonai and celebrate, honor, and proclaim His feast days. We don't have to celebrate other days that Adonai did not give us to celebrate and proclaim.

TURNING POINT:

Sukkot - A Time of Refreshing and Rejoicing Before Adonai

Leviticus 23:39-44 CJB

"'But on the fifteenth day of the seventh month, when you have gathered the produce of the land, you are to observe the festival of Adonai seven days; the first day is to be a complete rest and the eighth day is to be a complete rest. **40** On the first day you are to take **choice fruit**, **palm fronds**, **thick branches** and **river-willows**, and celebrate in the presence of Adonai your God for seven days. **41** You are to observe it as a feast to Adonai seven days in the year; it is a permanent regulation, generation after generation; keep it in the seventh month. **42** You are to live in sukkot for seven days; every citizen of Isra'el is to live in a sukkah, **43** so that generation after generation of you will know that I made the people of Isra'el live in sukkot when I brought them out of the land of Egypt; I am Adonai your God.'"

The ancient Jewish Rabbis teach that the four plant species that we wave in rejoicing show us the importance of unity within oneself and with others; and is also a symbol of our personalities. The choice fruit (Etrog/citron), is fragrant and tasty. It represents a person who knows the Torah and does good deeds. The palm fronds (Lulav), is a tasty fruit but has no smell. It represents a person who knows about the Torah but does not obey the words of the Torah. The Thick branches (Hadas), smell very good but have no taste. It represents a person who does not know the Torah but does good deeds. The river-willow branch (Arava) does not have any taste or smell. It represents a person who does not know the Torah or does any good deeds.[1] *(Stones Edition Chumash, page689)*

When we take these four plant species and hold them together it demonstrates the importance of the need for every one of us, those with strengths and weaknesses, for the One true God, the Creator of all things.

Which personal or type of plant species describes who you are?

Our aim as children of Adonai is to be the person who knows and obeys Torah, but does not neglect the one who is not.

Only in Yeshua can we truly live in obedience to the Torah and receive the refreshing of the Ruach HaKodesh (Holy Spirit).

John 7:37-40 TLV

"On the last and greatest day of the Feast, Yeshua stood up and cried out loudly, "If anyone is thirsty, let him come to Me and drink. Whoever believes in Me, as the Scripture says, 'out of his innermost being will flow rivers of living water.'" Now He said this about the Ruach, whom those who trusted in Him were going to receive; for the Ruach was not yet given, since Yeshua was not yet glorified. When they heard these words, some of the crowd said, "This man really is the Prophet."

PRACTICAL APPLICATIONS

Pray and ask the Ruach HaKodesh to give you the boldness to share with your friends about God's feasts that you celebrate. Tell your friends about your experience during Sukkot and Passover.

FOLLOW-UP FROM THE LAST TORAH PORTION

Ask who wants to share from last week's practical application

Responding in Obedience.

Purpose in your heart to respond in obedience to your parents, and or, your teachers immediately, so they do not have to tell you a second time what to do.

QUESTIONS - TEACHERS ANSWER KEY

1. The priest was only allowed to mourn for his *close relative*.

2. Who was the High Priest allowed to mourn for?
   No One

3. Give the names of the 8 feast days.
   Shabbat, Passover, Unleavened Bread, FirstFruits, Shavuot, Feast of Trumpets, Day of Atonement, Sukkot, and Shemini Atzeret

4. Which feast day is a weekly feast, and which feasts are yearly?
   Weekly: Shabbat **Yearly:** Passover, Unleavened Bread, FirstFruits, Shavuot, Feast of Trumpets, Day of Atonement, Sukkot, and Shemini Atzeret

5. How many loaves of bread were placed on the Table of Showbread?
   Twelve (12)

6. How often was the oil in the menorah replenished?
   Daily

7. In what two seasons of the year are the Feast days celebrated?
   Spring & Fall

8. What do the 12 loaves of Bread represent?
   12 Tribes of Israel

9. How old must an animal be for an acceptable offering?
   8 days old

10. Which feast day comes after counting the Omer?
    Shavuot

QUESTIONS - CHILDREN'S COPY

1. The priest was only allowed to mourn for his _____ _____.

2. Who was the High Priest allowed to mourn for?

3. Give the name of the 8 feast days.

4. Which feast day is a weekly feast, and which feasts are yearly?

5. How many loaves of bread were placed on the Table of Showbread?

6. How often was the oil in the menorah replenished?

7. In what two seasons of the year are the Feast days celebrated?

8. What do the 12 loaves of Bread represent?

9. How old must an animal be for an acceptable offering?

10. Which feast day comes after counting the Omer?

CRAFTS SUPPLIES FOR THE TORAH PORTION EMOR

CONTINUATION FROM LAST WEEK'S TORAH PORTION SUPPLIES:

1. 12x12" 2 Pieces of Cardstock Attached
2. Print color sheet templates
3. Markers/Pencils
4. Popsicle Sticks
5. Glue Sticks
6. Glue
7. Matzah Pieces
8. Fake Leaves
9. Leaves Stickers
10. Gems

*Color sheet templates are found on our website www.torah4children.net

CRAFTS: APPOINTED FEASTS OF ADONAI

Please note that this is a 2-WEEK PROJECT. Teachers, please continue with the craft project from the previous week. This week begins with step 6, if the children did not complete steps 1-5, allow a few minutes for them to do so.

1. Glue the Appointed feasts of Adonai and 7 branch menorah in the front of the craft booklet.

2. On the inside (left-hand side), create a door out of popsicle sticks, glue a drawing of lamb, and color it. Glue and color the Passover header.
3. Mark it on top and sides with a red marker to represent blood.
4. Next to it, glue the header Feast of Unleavened Bread and glue matzah under it.

5. Under Passover, glue header First Fruits and barley Under it.
6. Next to it, glue header Shavuot, and Torah drawing.

7. On the right side of the booklet, left corner, glue the header Yom Teruah and a man with a shofar drawing.
8. Next to it, glue the header Yom Kippur and Forbidden things under it.

9. On the bottom, glue the Sukkot header, and Sukkah drawing and color it. Put popsicle sticks around to represent Sukkah. Then fake leaves around it.

The Final Artwork

Behar/Beckhukotai

"On Mount Sinai/ By My Regulations"

Torah Portion 32 & 33:
Behar - Bechukotai "On Mount Sinai & By My Regulations"

Scripture Readings:

Behar — Leviticus 25:1-26:2, Jeremiah 32:6-27, Matthew 16:20-28, Psalm 112

Bechukotai — Leviticus 26:3-27:34, Jeremiah 16:19-17:14, John 14:15-21, Psalm 105

This week's Torah portion title consists of two Torah portions, Behar and Bechukotai. **"Behar"** is the Hebrew word that is translated as **"On Mount Sinai"** in Leviticus 25:1, and **Bechukotai** is the Hebrew word that means **"By My Regulations."** It is found in Leviticus 26:3.

Leviticus 25:1 NASB — The Lord then spoke to Moses **on Mount Sinai**, saying,

Leviticus 26:3 CJB — "'If you live by My regulations" observe My mitzvot and obey them;

The Theme of the Torah Portion:

Adonai Rulings and Teachings!

Scriptures for Theme

Leviticus 26: 46 CJB

These are the laws, rulings and teachings that *Adonai* himself gave to the people of Isra'el on Mount Sinai through Moshe.

Leviticus 27: 34 CJB

These are the mitzvot which Adonai gave to Moshe for the people of Isra'el on Mount Sinai.

Torah Portion Outline

- Sabbath Rest of the Land, **Leviticus 25:1-7**
- Jubilee, Year of Release, **Leviticus 25:8-20**
- Buying and Selling Land, **Leviticus 25:21-31**
- Cities of the Levites, **Leviticus 25:32-38**
- The Poor and the Foreigner, **Leviticus.25:39-54**
- Don't Bow to Idols, **Leviticus 26:1-2**
- Living to Please Adonai, **Leviticus 26:3-17**
- Discipline for Sin Against Adonai, **Leviticus 26:18-46**
- Making a Vow to Adonai, **Leviticus 27:1-15**
- Dedicating Land to Adonai, **Leviticus 27:16-25**
- The First Born Animals Belongs to Adonai, **Leviticus 27:26-29**
- The Tenth of Everything Belongs to Adonai, **Leviticus 27:30-34**

LESSON SUMMARY

Our Torah Portion for this week is another double portion. The Torah portion describes the commands Adonai gave to Moses for when the children of Israel enter the land He will be giving them. The land is to observe a sabbath rest unto Adonai. When they entered the land, for six years they were commanded to sow seeds and reap produce the land, but the seventh year was a complete rest for the land unto Adonai. The Lord then spoke to Moses at Mount Sinai, saying, "Speak to the sons of Israel and say to them, 'When you come into the land which I shall give you, then the land shall have a sabbath to the Lord. Six years you shall sow your field, and six years you shall prune your vineyard and gather in its crop, but during the seventh year the land shall have a sabbath rest, a sabbath to the Lord; you shall not sow your field nor prune your vineyard. **(Leviticus 25:1-4)**

They were also commanded to count seven sabbath years, that is forty-nine years; on Yom Kippur, they were to declare the fiftieth year a Jubilee, a complete rest and year of freedom for the land, the people, and the animals. This Jubilee year was consecrated to Adonai as holy because He is holy. It was proclaimed a Jubilee so that the people would not take advantage of each other. Adonai said to Moses; 'You are also to count off seven sabbaths of years for yourself, seven times seven years, so that you have the time of the seven sabbaths of years, namely, forty-nine years. You shall then sound a ram's horn abroad on the tenth day of the seventh month; on the day of atonement, you shall sound a horn all through your land. You shall thus consecrate the fiftieth year and proclaim a release through the land to all its inhabitants. It shall be a jubilee for you, and each of you shall return to his own property, and each of you shall return to his family. You shall have the fiftieth year as a jubilee; you shall not sow, nor reap its aftergrowth, nor gather in from its untrimmed vines. For it is a jubilee; it shall be holy to you. You shall eat its crops out of the field **(Leviticus 25:8-12)**.

Adonai gave the rulings for Moses to teach the people so that they would receive His blessings if they would obey and not cancel His covenant that He made with their forefathers, Abraham, Isaac, and Jacob. Adonai promised that the people would live safely in the land if they obeyed His command to let the land rest. The land would produce enough food in the sixth year to last for three years. However, if they chose not to obey His teachings, He would punish them for their sins severely. He would punish them so that the land would rest.

Commands and teachings were also given to anyone who wished to make a vow to Adonai. A vow could be from among the people, an animal (except the firstborn, it belongs to Adonai), a house, or a field. Each vow is consecrated as holy and given according to its acceptable value set by Adonai or the priest. Adonai declared the tenth of all things belongs to Him. The seeds or fruits from a tree, and animals from the herds or flock.

LESSON DISCUSSION

I Will Remember My Covenant!

Adonai gave Moses instructions for when the people enter the land He will be giving them. He also told Moses to let them know His rulings for when they obey His commands for the land and how He would discipline them if they chose not to obey. Sabbath is for Adonai whether it is the land or the people resting (Leviticus 25:1-7). The children of Israel were also commanded to count seven sabbaths of years up to forty-nine years, The Fiftieth year was to be a Jubilee, a year of release and sabbath rest for the land. (Leviticus 25:8-12)

Adonai told Moses the people will be blessed if they obey His commands.

Leviticus 26: 3-6,11 & 12 — "If you live by my regulations, observe my mitzvot (commands) and obey them; 4 then I will provide the rain you need in its season, the land will yield its produce, and the trees in the field will yield their fruit. 5 Your threshing time will extend until the grape harvest, and your grape harvesting will extend until the time for sowing seed. You will eat as much food as you want and live securely in your land. I will give shalom in the land — you will lie down to sleep unafraid of anyone. 6 I will rid the land of wild animals. 11 I will put my tabernacle among you, and I will not reject you, 12 but I will walk among you and be your God, and you will be my people.

If they chose to disobey and cancel His covenant He made with their forefathers, He would punish them for their sins if they did not allow the land to rest.

Adonai declares; "But if you will not listen to me and obey all these mitzvot, if you loathe my regulations and reject my rulings, in order not to obey all my mitzvot but cancel my covenant; then I, for my part, will do this to you: I will bring terror upon you — wasting disease and chronic fever to dim your sight and sap your strength. You will sow your seed for nothing, because your enemies will eat the crops. I will set my face against you — your enemies will defeat you, those who hate you will hound you, and you will flee when no one is pursuing you" (Leviticus 26:14-17).

This was only the beginning of what Adonai would do to the people. If they continued to disobey, He would punish them severely seven times, over and over. He would even allow their enemies to take them away from the land so the land would have its sabbath rest. But when they confessed their sins and repented, Adonai would remember them, because of the covenant He made with their forefathers. Adonai promised to restore His people and the land.

Remembering the Covenant and Restoring the People
Leviticus 26:40-46 — But if they confess their and their ancestors' guilt for the wrongdoing they did to me, and for their continued opposition to me— **41** which made me oppose them, so I took them into enemy territory—or if their uncircumcised hearts are humbled and they make up for their guilt, **42** then I will remember my covenant with Jacob. I will also remember my covenant with Isaac. And my covenant with Abraham. And I will remember the land. **43** The land will be absent of them and will be enjoying its sabbaths while it lies devastated, free of them. They will be making up for their guilty deeds for no other reason than the fact that they rejected my regulations and despised my rules. **44** But despite all that, when they are in enemy territory, I will not reject them or despise them to the point of totally destroying them, breaking my covenant with them by doing so, because I am the Lord their God. **45** But for their sake I will remember the covenant with the first generation, the ones I brought out of Egypt's land in the sight of all the nations, to be their God; I am the Lord.

Adonai only punishes us when we disobey His commands.
If they refused to obey, He would allow their enemies to take them out of the land. This reminds us of when Adam and Eve disobeyed God and He drove them out of the garden.

God always remembers His covenant. We too can inherit the blessings promised in the covenant if we believe in Yeshua. When we disobey God's command, if we confess and repent of our sin He will restore our relationship with Him.

Galatians 3:29 CJB — "If you belong to the Messiah (Yeshua the anointed One), you are seed of Avraham (Abraham) and heirs according to the promise.

Acts 2:38-39 THE MESSAGE TRANSLATION
Peter said, "Change your life. Turn to God and be baptized, each of you, in the name of Jesus Christ, so your sins are forgiven. Receive the gift of the Holy Spirit. The promise is targeted to you and your children, but also to all who are far away—whomever, in fact, our Master God invites."

WE HAVE COMPLETED ANOTHER BOOK OF THE TORAH SO WE DECLARE

Chazak, Chazak, V'nit'chazek!
Be Strong, Be Strong, And Let Us Be Strengthened!

TURNING POINT:

WALK UPRIGHT

In this week's Torah readings, Adonai gave Moses His rulings for the people once they entered the land He promised to give them. He commanded that they should allow the land to observe a sabbath rest every seven years, and to declare a Jubilee, a year of release for the people and the land every fifty years. During the Jubilee year, each person who had to sell their property because of debt would return to his property. Adonai's rulings for the Jubilee were so that the people would not treat each other like they were in Egypt. He pronounced His blessings the people would receive if they obeyed His regulations and all the punishment they would endure if they chose to disobey.

Leviticus 26:12-13 — I will walk among you and will be your God, and you will be My people. **13** I am Adonai your God, who brought you forth out of the land of Egypt, so that you would not be their slaves, and I have broken the bars of your yoke and made you walk upright.

You are not a slave to any nation or person, but did you know that when we choose to disobey God you become a slave to your sin?

The Apostle Paul writes in Romans 6:16; "Don't you know that if you offer yourselves to someone as obedient slaves, that you are slaves of the one whom you obey? That's true whether you serve as slaves of sin, which leads to death, or as slaves of the kind of obedience that leads to righteousness."

Adonai broke the yoke (the burden of slavery) from the children of Israel so they could walk upright, to walk in as His children, and in freedom to His commands. They had to learn God's commands to walk in His freedom. You too can walk in freedom, Yeshua declares "Take my yoke upon you and learn from me, for I am gentle and humble in heart, and you will find rest for your souls" (Matthew 11:29).

Are you willing to learn Adonai's ways so you can walk upright?

PRACTICAL APPLICATIONS

FOR CHILDREN 4-6 YEARS OLD
Put away your favorite toys for the next 7 days.

FOR CHILDREN 7-12 YEARS OLD

LEARN TO SPEAK A BLESSING OTHERS

Ask your family members or friends if they follow God's commands. If they answer yes, say, May the Lord bless and keep you!

If they answer no, then ask, "Would you like to pray and ask God to forgive your sins and accept Yeshua?

FOLLOW-UP FROM THE LAST TORAH PORTION

Ask who wants to share from last week's practical application

Pray and ask the Ruach HaKodesh to give you the boldness to share with your friends about God's feasts that you celebrate. Tell your friends about your experience during Sukkot and Passover.

QUESTIONS - TEACHERS ANSWER KEY

1. **What feast should the land keep unto Adonai?**
   Sabbath

2. **What are two things the people are commanded to do for six years?**
   Sow seeds, prune, and reap crops

3. **Every fiftieth year from the forty-ninth sabbath year is declared a <u>Jubilee</u>!**

4. **On what day and month is the Jubilee declared?**
   On the tenth day of the seventh month

5. **What were the people commanded to do to consecrate the Jubilee to Adonai?**
   Blow the shofar

6. **Which feast day is also on the tenth day of the seventh month?**
   Day of Atonement (Yom Kippur)

7. **Give three promises for obedience.**
   Rain, protection, peace, fruitfulness (see Lev.26:3-13)

8. **Give three punishments for disobedience.**
   Sickness, disease, death (See Lev.26:14-39)

9. **For whose sake will Adonai remember His covenant?**
   Abraham, Isaac, and Jacob

10. **What is another name for Jubilee?**
    The Year of Release

QUESTIONS - CHILDREN'S COPY

1. What feast should the land keep unto Adonai?

2. What are two things the people are commanded to do for six years?

3. Every fiftieth year from the forty-ninth sabbath year is declared a _____!

4. On what day and month is the Jubilee declared?

5. What were the people commanded to do to consecrate the Jubilee to Adonai?

6. Which feast day is also on the tenth day of the seventh month?

7. Give three promises for obedience according to Leviticus 26:3-13.

8. Give three punishments for disobedience according to Leviticus 26:3-13.

9. For whose sake will Adonai remember His covenant?

10. What is another name for Jubilee?

CRAFTS SUPPLIES FOR THE TORAH PORTION BEHAR-BECHUKOTAI

SUPPLIES:
1. 12x12" Cardstock of Various Colors
2. Green Construction Paper
3. Brown Cardstock
4. Green Felt Paper
5. Apple or Any Tree Fruit Stickers
6. Rain Drop Stickers
7. Markers/Pencils
8. Glue Sticks
9. Cotton Balls

CRAFT: BLESSINGS FOR OBEDIENCE

1. On 12x12" cardstock, glue green strips of construction paper on the bottom of the page to represent grass.
2. In the middle bottom of the page, glue pre-cut brown cardstock to represent the tree.

3. Glue pre-cut green felt on top of the green construction paper to represent the tree leaves. Stick apple stickers as shown.

4. On the top left corner, take raindrop stickers and glue just a few to represent raindrops. Then add with blue pencil the rest of the rain drops.
5. Glue cotton balls in the corner to represent the cloud.

6. Color the man with his wife and baby and glue it on the left bottom corner.
7. Color words "Blessings for Obedience" and glue them as shown.
8. Color all the blessings and glue them as shown.

The Completed work

About the Authors

Natalee Henry began her personal faith journey in 1996 with a burning desire to live an extraordinary life for the Lord. Since then, the Lord has kindled a passion within her for sharing and teaching the Word of God.

In 2016, God answered Natalee's prayer for spiritual growth when she was introduced to studying, learning, and implementing the Torah way of life as a believer in Yeshua. Natalee is a Torah-observant believer learning to honor God's Appointed Times and serving within her local congregation to all ages.

Natalee is an author, motivational speaker, and founder of the Season Destiny Ministry designed to "*empower youths to make the right decisions in life.*" Natalee is a graduate of International Seminary Bible College, and authored *Seasons of Life-Taking Man Back To God*, 2005; *Embracing Destiny*, 2010; *Overcome to Fulfill Your Purpose: Become Successfully You*, and *Successfully You, Leadership Training Workbook* 2018, and her most recent, *Making Transition Through Crisis: A Rebuilding Guide for Young Professionals*, 2021.

Natalee has a passion for young people and seeks to share with them that they do not have to 'settle' for being less than God created them to be; nor do they need to succumb to today's culture, lies, and worldliness.

 **Yevgeniya Calendrillo** was born and raised in Ukraine to a secular Jewish family. Growing up, Yevgeniya yearned for a relationship with God for many years. By the age of 24, she was married and living in the United States. Yevgeniya and her husband are entrepreneurs and business partners selling their artwork and also are heavily focused on nutrition and health. Yevgeniya and her husband have one son, whom she homeschooled for 3 1/2 years.

Yevgeniya was invited to a Messianic congregation in Brooklyn where she accepted Yeshua as her Savior; and opened the Bible for the very first time. Yevgeniya has been a Messianic believer for over 20 years.

Yevgniya has a Bachelor's degree in Fashion Design from the Fashion Institute of Technology, New York. Yevgeniya has many years of experience in the New York fashion industry. Yevgniya is an artist who is gifted in watercolor painting. She recently discovered her talent for children's crafts and utilizes her knowledge, and experience in arts and design, as tools for investing in children for the Kingdom of God. Yevgeniya is currently serving as Children's Ministry Leader and a children's Torah teacher at Save The Nations.

Yevgeniya has a passion to follow God, to be obedient to His Torah instructions, to seek Him diligently, and to walk in her calling to teach Torah and Hebrew lessons to children.

About the Book

Vayikra (Book 3: Leviticus) is a part of the Torah Curriculum for children, covering the first five books of the Bible. This curriculum is based on the weekly Torah Portions so they may learn Torah in a simple and practical way.

The Lessons are structured so our children will learn from the Torah Portions and see the connection with Yeshua (Jesus), and the work of the Holy Spirit. Our aim is not just to give information but to teach Torah principles and demonstrate how to use them in their lives.

Each lesson is designed as a guide for teaching the Torah Portions to children ages 4 to 12 years. This curriculum is filled with creative crafts designed by Yevgeniya and insightful lessons written by Natalee.

Visit our website at www.torah4children.net to learn more about other books from our curriculum and our ministry.

www.ingramcontent.com/pod-product-compliance
Lightning Source LLC
Chambersburg PA
CBHW060235240426
43663CB00041B/2898